# Homes Through *Time*

Julie Haydon

## Contents

# Chapter 1

# People on the Move

Long ago people did not live in one place. They followed the animals they **hunted**. The people did not know how to grow their own food. They did not know how to keep farm animals.

Sometimes the people lived in caves. Sometimes they made homes out of the **materials** they found around them. The homes were easy to put up and take down, like tents today.

The first homes were made from animal skins, wood, leaves, grasses, bones, and **tusks**.

# Chapter 2

# The First Villages

People learned to grow **crops**. They learned how to keep animals for food. Now they could live in one place all the time.

People built houses in groups. These groups of houses were the first villages. People needed water. Many villages were built near a river or lake.

People learned to make bricks from mud. In some places, houses were made from stone or wood.

# Chapter 3

# Towns in Egypt

People built villages in Egypt a long time ago. The villages were along the **Nile River**. The people made their houses from bricks of mud and straw. The bricks were left in the sun to dry. The houses had flat roofs where people could play and rest.

The Nile River flooded every year. It left behind rich mud. The mud kept the soil healthy. The people grew crops in the soil. Some of the villages got larger. Soon they were towns.

The houses in Egypt had only a few windows. This helped to keep the hot sun out.

# Chapter 4

# Apartments in Rome

Over time cities were built. Many people lived in the city of Rome. Rich people lived in nice houses with gardens. Many other people lived in apartment buildings.

Some apartment buildings were not safe. Sometimes they fell down. People cooked in their apartments and burned fires to stay warm. Sometimes this started a fire in a building.

There were often shops on the ground floors of the apartment buildings.

# Chapter 5

# A Viking Village

The **Vikings** were a people who lived long ago. They lived in villages in very cold places. The men often sailed to other places in their ships.

Viking houses were made of wood. Some houses had walls made of sticks and clay. Most Viking houses had just one room. People cooked, ate, slept, and worked in the room.

Viking houses had roofs made of wooden tiles or of **thatch**.

# Chapter 6

# Castles

The first castles were made of wood. They were built on the top of **man-made** hills. A strong wooden wall went around the castle. Later, stone castles were built.

The middle part of the castle was called the keep. There was land outside the keep. This land was called the bailey. Strong walls were built around the keep and the bailey. The walls helped to keep out enemies.

Sometimes a ditch was dug around a castle. A ditch that was full of water was called a moat.

# Chapter 7

# Life in a Yurt

More people started to live in cities. However, a people called the **Mongols** lived in tents. Their tents were called yurts.

The Mongols kept animals like cows, goats, and sheep. They rode horses. The animals needed plants to eat. The Mongols moved from place to place to find food for their animals.

Yurts were made of felt and had a wooden frame. Some Mongols still live in yurts today.

# Chapter 8

# Houses Near Factories

Over time factories were built. Most factories were built in cities and towns. Many factories were near **coal mines**. There were machines in the factories. Coal was burned to make power for the machines.

People were needed to work in the factories. The people needed houses. Lots of houses were built very quickly. The houses were often small and dark. Many of the houses were built close together.

The factories made lots of coal smoke. This made the houses near the factories very dirty.

# Chapter 9
# Homes Today

Today many people live in large cities. Homes in cities are often made of brick or **concrete**.

Many homes have:

- lots of rooms

- lots of windows to let in light

- many machines

- heating

- hot and cold water

- electricity

Many homes today have a garage and a yard.

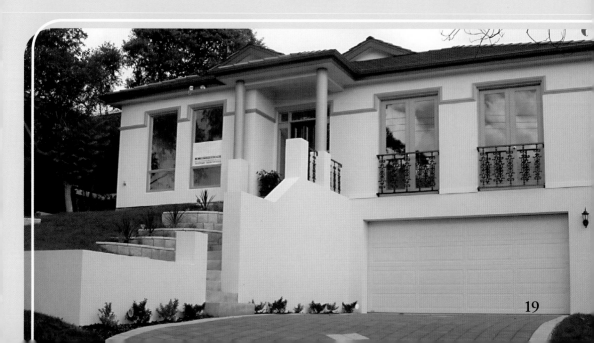

# Chapter 10

# Homes in the Future

In the future, there will be more people. People may have to build houses on smaller pieces of land. There may be more apartment buildings.

Computers may be used to run our homes. Better machines will do a lot of the work in our houses.

Astronauts can live for months on **space stations** and **spacecraft**. In the future, homes may even be built on the moon! People need air to breathe. There is no air on the moon. Homes on the moon will need machines that make air.

# Chapter 11

# Homes Around the World

Here are some other homes around the world today.

a houseboat in France

a stone cottage in Britain

a castle in France

a stilt house in Thailand

# Glossary

| | |
|---|---|
| **coal** | a hard, dark material found in the earth that can burn |
| **concrete** | a building material that is hard and strong when it dries |
| **crops** | plants that people grow for food |
| **hunted** | caught and killed for food |
| **man-made** | made by people |
| **materials** | things made up of different substances |
| **mines** | holes in the earth that people dig to look for rocks |
| **Mongols** | a people living in a country called Mongolia in Asia |
| **Nile River** | a large river in Africa |
| **spacecraft** | machines that can fly in space |
| **space stations** | places where astronauts can live and work in space |
| **thatch** | a roof covering made of straw, reeds, or leaves |
| **tusks** | very long teeth on some animals |
| **Vikings** | a people who lived in northern Europe a long time ago |

# Index